HACKS OF LIFE

300 + LIFE HACKS YOU WISH YOU HAD KNOWN SOONER

Published by Willow Creek Press, Inc.
P.O. Box 147, Minocqua, Wisconsin 54548

This book is provided for general informational purposes only. The tips, tricks, and hacks contained within this book are intended to offer alternatives and shortcuts for a variety of everyday tasks and challenges. While we strive to ensure the information is accurate and useful, we make no representations or warranties of any kind, express or implied, about the completeness, accuracy, reliability, suitability, or availability with respect to this book or the information, products, services, or related graphics contained in this book for any purpose.

The hacks provided should be used as a guide and adapted to individual needs and circumstances. Before attempting any hack that involves tools, chemicals, or could potentially impact your health or safety, professional advice should be sought. The authors, publishers, and contributors cannot be held responsible for any injury, harm, or damage to property that may result from the application of hacks and advice contained within.

Printed in the United States

HACKS OF LIFE

300 + LIFE HACKS YOU WISH YOU HAD KNOWN SOONER

WILLOW CREEK PRESS®

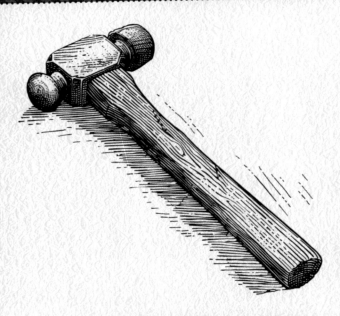

GLUE A MAGNET TO THE BOTTOM OF YOUR HAMMER TO HOLD A FEW NAILS.

By gluing a magnet at the end of your hammer handle, you have a hands-free way to pick up and hold nails— perfect for when you need them.

IF THE ZIPPER ON YOUR PANTS WON'T STAY UP, USE A HAIR TIE LOOPED THROUGH THE BUTTON HOLE AS A WAISTBAND EXTENDER.

A MIX OF EQUAL PARTS OF DISH SOAP AND VINEGAR IN A SPRAY BOTTLE WILL EASILY CLEAN DIRTY GLASS SHOWER DOORS.

TO EASE HARD WATER BUILDUP, USE A RUBBER BAND TO SECURE A PLASTIC BAG FULL OF WHITE VINEGAR TO YOUR SHOWER HEAD OVERNIGHT.

PLACING YOUR PHONE IN A GLASS CUP WILL AMPLIFY THE SOUND.

When you put your phone in a glass or porcelain cup, the sound waves bounce around a little and are directed up and out, amplifying the volume a small amount.

OVER-THE-DOOR SHOE ORGANIZERS CAN ALSO BE USED FOR STORING AND ORGANIZING YOUR BOTTLES OF CLEANING SUPPLIES.

A BREAD TAB CAN HELP HOLD THE SPOT ON A ROLL OF TAPE.

NEED A RELIABLE SOURCE? TRY USING GOOGLE SCHOLAR INSTEAD OF GOOGLE FOR PEER-REVIEWED ARTICLES.

CASSEROLES OF ANY TYPE WILL PROVIDE MANY SERVINGS WHILE KEEPING COSTS AND EFFORT LOW.

GET RID OF MICE BY PLACING STROBE LIGHTS IN YOUR GARAGE OR ATTIC.

Setting a timer for the lights to go off at certain times of the day may help with deterring them from your home.

NERVOUS ABOUT SELLING SOMETHING TO A COMPLETE STRANGER? ARRANGE TO MEET UP AT A POLICE STATION.

USE A HEATED BLANKET DURING THE WINTER MONTHS INSTEAD OF A SPACE HEATER TO KEEP WARM. HEATED BLANKETS USE LESS ENERGY THAN SPACE HEATERS.

DIRTY SCREEN DOORS? ROLL A LINT ROLLER OVER THE SCREEN TO CLEAN IT.

FREEZE LEFTOVER SOUP STOCK IN AN ICE
CUBE TRAY. WHEN YOU'RE READY TO USE
SOME, REHEAT IT IN A SAUCE PAN.

KETCHUP CAN BE USED TO CLEAN COPPER ITEMS.

Apply a layer of ketchup to a copper pan or copper sink, and rub the condiment all over the surface. The tomatoes in ketchup contain an acid that helps remove tarnish. Rinse and dry.

LIGHT MULTIPLE CANDLES USING A STRAND OF SPAGHETTI RATHER THAN BURNING THROUGH INDIVIDUAL MATCHES.

DAYTIME NAPS HAVE BEEN PROVEN TO CUT THE RISK OF HEART DISEASES AND ALSO IMPROVE SHORT-TERM MEMORY.

One study found that naps of approximately 20 minutes improved the overall mood of participants. However, longer naps lasting more than 30 minutes are not typically associated with improved mood and increased feelings of well-being. Short naps may also be associated with a reduced risk of cardiovascular diseases.

LOWER YOUR CHOLESTEROL BY EATING UNSALTED SUNFLOWER SEEDS.

USE DENTAL FLOSS TO CLEANLY CUT THROUGH LOGS OF SOFT CHEESE.

HAIR STRAIGHTENERS CAN IRON OUT THOSE WRINKLES IN CLOTHES!

Straighteners are great for quickly removing wrinkles in your collared shirt or blouse. Start by cleaning the straightener to remove any remaining hair products. It is also essential to be aware of your temperature settings. Cotton needs high heat, and silk needs low heat. Next, pull the piece of clothing tight and run the straightener a few times along the section you want to smooth out. Move the straightener fast so that your clothing doesn't get burnt. Hair straighteners work great on collars, cuffs and hems.

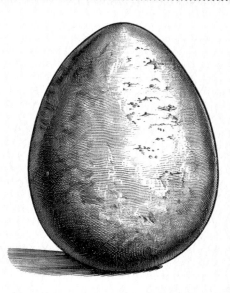

CAN'T FIND THE EXPIRATION DATE OF YOUR EGGS? IF YOUR EGGS FLOAT IN A GLASS OF WATER, THEY ARE EXPIRED.

PIERCE A STRAW THROUGH THE MIDDLE OF A STRAWBERRY TO REMOVE THE STEM.

A plastic or metal straw is all you need for this trick. Stick your straw into the bottom of the fruit until you pierce a hole in it. Then, use the straw to channel through the strawberry until you reach the head. With a final push, you'll be able to remove the leaves.

PLACING A SCENTED DRYER SHEET IN EACH SHOE OVERNIGHT CAN HELP THEM SMELL FRESH THE NEXT DAY.

A PERMANENT MARKER STAIN ON FURNITURE CAN BE ERASED BY USING RUBBING ALCOHOL.

ACNE BREAKING OUT REGULARLY? TRY CHANGING YOUR PILLOWCASES DAILY.

USE PACKING CUBES TO KEEP YOUR CLOTHING ORGANIZED AND WRINKLE-FREE IN YOUR LUGGAGE.

PLACING NEWSPAPERS AT THE BOTTOM OF A TRASH CAN CAN HELP ABSORB FOOD LIQUIDS AND OILS.

CUT PERFECT POTATO WEDGES WITH AN APPLE SLICER.

DIRTY MICROWAVE? MIX WATER, LEMON JUICE, AND VINEGAR IN A MICROWAVE-SAFE CONTAINER. MICROWAVE UNTIL IT STEAMS UP. WIPE THE RESIDUE AWAY EASILY.

BRAIN FREEZE? PRESSING THE BACK OF YOUR TONGUE AGAINST THE SOFT PALATE OF YOUR MOUTH WILL HELP THE FREEZE GO AWAY.

STOCK YOUR OFFICE OR DESK WITH SNACKS AND GOODIES. THIS WILL HELP KEEP YOU FROM SPENDING AT THE VENDING MACHINE.

CHEW SOME GUM WHILE CUTTING ONIONS IF CUTTING THEM MAKES YOU CRY. CHEWING HELPS DIFFUSE ODORS.

FEELING STRESSED? TAKE A MOMENT TO TAKE DEEP BREATHS.

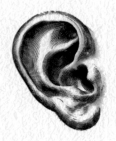

SLOWLY MASSAGING YOUR EARLOBES WILL SLOWLY ALLEVIATE HEADACHES.

THROW YOUR PILLOWS IN THE DRYER TO HELP FLUFF THEM BACK UP.

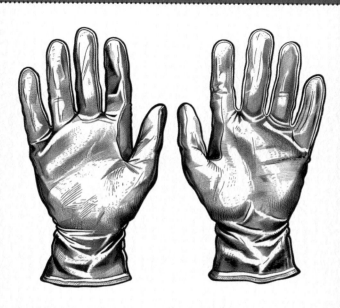

PUTTING ON A RUBBER GLOVE CAN
HELP YOU OPEN STUCK JAR TOPS.

USE EMPTY TOILET PAPER ROLLS
TO HELP KEEP YOUR CABLES
AND CORDS ORGANIZED.

PUT LEMON JUICE ON YOUR APPLE SLICES TO KEEP THEM FROM OXIDIZING FOR A COUPLE DAYS.

The longer the enzyme is exposed, the browner each slice will become. Lemon juice contains citric acid, which is a natural antioxidant. Therefore, when you apply lemon juice to apple slices, it helps to prevent the oxidation process.

IF YOU ACCIDENTALLY CLOSE A TAB IN YOUR INTERNET BROWSER, YOU CAN RETRIEVE IT BY HOLDING DOWN CTRL + SHIFT + T.

REVIVE STALE BREAD BY WRAPPING IT IN A DAMP TOWEL AND BAKING BRIEFLY.

TO PREVENT YOUR BATHROOM MIRROR FROM FOGGING OVER, BUFF CAR WAX INTO THE GLASS USING A SOFT, DRY CLOTH.

TO AVOID CRAMPS WHILE RUNNING, TRY TO EXHALE WHEN YOUR LEFT FOOT STRIKES THE GROUND.

NEED TO CHARGE YOUR PHONE? PUT IT IN AIRPLANE MODE FOR A QUICKER BATTERY BOOST.

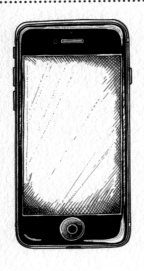

While airplane mode doesn't actually make your device charge faster, it does restrict what the device is doing, which may cut down on energy-intensive processes.

MAKE YOUR DIRTY SHOES LOOK CLEAN AGAIN BY REMOVING THE DIRT AND DEBRIS WITH TOOTHPASTE.

Use either a toothbrush or a cleaning pad to scrub the dirt from the shoes. Let the toothpaste dry into the shoes before removing it with a damp cloth and a water and soap solution.

TOO MUCH SALT IN YOUR SOUP?
ADD CUBED POTATOES TO IT;
THEY'LL ABSORB THE SALT.

KEEPING INDOOR PLANTS HEALTHY CAN BE A CHORE. CREATE A WEEKLY WATERING SCHEDULE.

YOU CAN CONNECT TWO ZIPLOC BAGS BY FLIPPING ONE INSIDE OUT TO MAKE A LARGER ONE.

PACK A FULL SET OF CLOTHES IN YOUR CARRY-ON IN CASE YOUR CHECKED LUGGAGE GETS LOST BY THE AIRLINE.

NO-SCREEN SUNDAYS: DEDICATE A DAY TO UNPLUGGING EACH WEEK.

IF IT TAKES LESS THAN TWO MINUTES, DO IT NOW.

CHECK A VEHICLE'S HISTORY BEFORE BUYING A PRE-OWNED VEHICLE. WEBSITES SUCH AS CARFAX ARE GREAT RESOURCES.

NEED TO KILL OFF WEEDS BETWEEN CRACKS IN YOUR DRIVEWAY OR SIDEWALK? POURING BOILING WATER ON WEEDS WILL KILL THEM.

Pouring boiling water on weeds can be used especially in situations where other plants are not nearby, such as in cracks in patios or sidewalks. Boiling water will act as a contact "herbicide," killing only the portion of the plant it comes in contact with. It is most effective on young, newly emerged weeds.

RUBBING A WALNUT OVER SCRATCHES AND IMPERFECTIONS IN YOUR FURNITURE WILL COVER THEM UP.

Rub a raw walnut back and forth diagonally across the length of a scratch for a few seconds, then use a soft microfiber cloth and gently buff out the scratched area.

STORE YOUR CAN OPENER IN
THE FREEZER TO PREVENT
IT FROM RUSTING.

USE OVERRIPE BANANAS TO BAKE A LOAF OF BANANA BREAD.

WEB BROWSERS CAN SET WEBSITES AND YOUR FREQUENTLY USED ONLINE TOOLS TO AUTOMATICALLY OPEN AT STARTUP.

KEEP A CARD WITH IMPORTANT MEDICAL INFORMATION AND PHONE NUMBERS IN YOUR WALLET OR PURSE. IT COULD SAVE YOUR LIFE.

TRAVELING INTERNATIONALLY? PURCHASE A PASSPORT HOLDER OR BAG TO KEEP ALL YOUR IMPORTANT DOCUMENTS IN ONE PLACE.

USE A HAIR DRYER TO WARM AN AREA WITH A STICKER THAT YOU NEED TO REMOVE.

BRING SOME LINT WITH YOU ON YOUR NEXT CAMPING TRIP. LINT IS A GREAT WAY TO HELP IGNITE AND KEEP A FIRE GOING.

EVERY 20 MINUTES, LOOK AT SOMETHING 20 FEET AWAY FOR 20 SECONDS TO REDUCE EYE STRAIN.

START A GRATITUDE JOURNAL: LIST THREE THINGS YOU'RE GRATEFUL FOR EACH DAY.

PICK ONE DAY DURING THE WEEK TO TREAT YOURSELF. DO ANYTHING YOU WANT, EAT ANYTHING YOU WANT, AND ENJOY IT.

WATER BEFORE COFFEE: DRINK A GLASS OF WATER EACH MORNING BEFORE CAFFEINE.

The very first reason why we must drink water before caffeinated beverages is that it hydrates the whole body. Many people believe that tea and coffee actually rejuvenate the body, but instead, they dehydrate the body from the inside.

WANT TO WATCH JUST ONE OR TWO FILMS FROM A STREAMING SERVICE? MANY OF THEM OFFER FREE TRIALS WITHOUT EVER CHARGING.

WRAP RUBBER BANDS AROUND JAR LIDS FOR EASIER OPENING.

LEAVING A DAB OF SHAVING CREAM ON A PESKY CLOTHES STAIN OVERNIGHT WILL HELP REMOVE IT EASILY.

PLACE MONEY IN A MARKED ENVELOPE TO BUDGET. USE ONLY WHAT IS AVAILABLE IN EACH ENVELOPE FOR EACH EXPENSE.

Cash stuffing is essentially a modern term for the straightforward budgeting technique commonly referred to as "envelope budgeting" or the "envelope system." This method entails allocating cash into labeled envelopes for various spending categories and limiting your expenditures to the amount designated for each month.

OLIVE OIL CAN BE A GOOD SUBSTITUTE FOR SHAVING CREAM.

Olive oil has been used for centuries as a natural moisturizer. Rich in antioxidants and nourishing for skin, olive oil is a healthier alternative to shaving creams, which are often filled with artificial scents and chemicals that leave skin itchy and dry.

KEEP A FEW PLANTS IN YOUR OFFICE OR WORKSPACE. STUDIES HAVE SHOWN THAT PLANTS CAN HELP PEOPLE RELAX.

A DASH OF SALT ON A NAPKIN WILL KEEP YOUR CUP FROM STICKING TO IT.

STUCK DRAWERS CAN BE FIXED BY RUBBING DOWN THE TRACK WITH SOME SOAP.

A WEIGHTED BLANKET CAN HELP CALM AND RELAX YOU AFTER A LONG DAY.

TIRED OF SEEING ADS TARGETING YOU? CONDUCT ALL YOUR ONLINE SHOPPING IN A PRIVATE OR INCOGNITO BROWSER WINDOW.

FLOSS BEFORE BRUSHING. THIS WILL HELP LOOSEN UP THE PLAQUE AND DEBRIS IN YOUR MOUTH.

A study has found that flossing first followed by brushing with a fluoride toothpaste is more effective in removing interdental plaque than brushing first, flossing second. In addition, flossing before brushing results in greater fluoride retention between teeth.

PEELING A BANANA FROM THE
BOTTOM IS EASIER THAN
PEELING FROM THE TOP.

EAT VEGGIES OR A HEALTHY APPETIZER
BEFORE DIGGING INTO THE MAIN COURSE.
THIS WILL HELP FILL YOU UP ON FIBER.

FORGET WHICH SIDE YOUR GAS TANK IS ON? YOUR GAS LEVEL INDICATOR HAS AN ARROW POINTING TO WHICH SIDE IT IS ON.

USE A CHEESE GRATER TO SOFTEN COLD BUTTER.

HANGING CLOTHES UP IN A ROOM TO DRY? TURN ON A FAN IN THE ROOM TO HELP DRY THEM QUICKER.

EATING A SPOONFUL OF PEANUT BUTTER CAN HELP ALLEVIATE HICCUPS.

GOING ON A TRIP FOR A WEEK OR LONGER? HAVE THE POST OFFICE HOLD YOUR MAIL FOR YOU WHILE YOU ARE GONE.

USPS Hold Mail service can hold your mail safely at your local Post Office facility until you return, for up to 30 days.

JOIN LOCAL CLUBS AND GROUPS TO ENRICH YOUR LIFE WITH THE HOBBIES AND INTERESTS YOU ENJOY.

FULL FRIDGES USE LESS ENERGY TO KEEP COOL.

A full fridge will generally consume less energy than an empty one. This is because the items in a full fridge help to maintain the cold temperature when the door is opened, reducing the amount of warm air that enters. An empty fridge, on the other hand, requires more energy to cool the empty space and to maintain the cold temperature.

MAKING YOUR BED EVERY MORNING WILL HELP YOUR ROOM FEEL MORE TIDY AND ORGANIZED.

Making your bed can improve your mood and productivity, and create a sense of accomplishment to start your day. It only takes a few minutes to make your bed, and the benefits can last all day.

WHITE WINE CAN HELP
REMOVE RED WINE STAINS.

A MAKEUP BRUSH CAN HELP CLEAN A KEYBOARD.

COMMAND HOOKS AND 3M STRIPS ARE GREAT WAYS TO KEEP YOUR WALLS PUNCTURE FREE.

ONIONS AND GARLIC HELP ACCELERATE HAIR GROWTH.

STORE CANNED FOODS SUCH AS BAKED BEANS UPSIDE DOWN. THIS WILL ELIMINATE THE NEED TO SCRAPE THEM OUT FROM THE BOTTOM.

THREADING YOUR NECKLACES THROUGH A STRAW WILL HELP KEEP THEM TANGLE-FREE.

A MIX OF WATER AND PEPPERMINT OIL AROUND WINDOW SILLS AND DOORS CAN KEEP SPIDERS AWAY.

TAKE ADVANTAGE OF STORE REWARDS PROGRAMS TO EARN POINTS AND SAVE MONEY.

NEED A BOOKMARK? USE A PAPER CLIP TO MARK YOUR SPOT!

CHECK WITH YOUR CREDIT CARD COMPANY TO SEE IF YOUR CARD GIVES YOU ACCESS TO AIRPORT LOUNGES.

DIRTY OVEN AND PANS? USE A MIX OF BAKING SODA AND VINEGAR TO CLEAN THEM.

COOKING AN EXTRA SERVING OF FOOD FOR DINNER CAN MEAN LUNCH FOR THE NEXT DAY!

TURN OFF SOCIAL MEDIA NOTIFICATIONS DURING THE DAY. THIS WILL HELP KEEP YOU FROM BEING DISTRACTED.

When you have notifications constantly bombarding you, it can feel like you have to respond to everything right now. With them off, it's amazing what falls away.

A TEASPOON OF BAKING SODA WILL HELP HARD-BOILED EGGS PEEL EASIER.

Adding a teaspoon of baking soda to the water when boiling eggs can help make the shells easier to peel. The alkaline nature of the baking soda can help to break down the proteins in the egg whites, making the shells less likely to stick to the eggs.

USE TWO LAUNDRY HAMPERS TO
KEEP YOUR LAUNDRY SEPARATED
AND ORGANIZED BEFORE WASHING IT.

TAKE A NAP. A QUICK NAP CAN HELP REJUVENATE YOUR ENERGY LEVELS.

PAINTING YOUR LIGHT SWITCHES AND CHARGING CORDS WITH GLOW-IN-THE-DARK PAINT CAN HELP YOU SEE THEM IN THE DARK.

PICK A DESIGNATED SPOT FOR YOUR MOST IMPORTANT ITEMS TO KEEP FROM LOSING THEM. YOU'RE MORE LIKELY TO PLACE THEM THERE OUT OF HABIT.

WHEN LOOKING FOR A NEW HOME OR APARTMENT, CHECK YOUR CELL PHONE SIGNAL STRENGTH BEFORE MAKING A DECISION.

WRITE THE EMAIL FIRST THEN ADD THE RECIPIENTS. THIS WILL SAVE YOU FROM ACCIDENTALLY SENDING AN EMAIL PREMATURELY!

SECURE TRASH BAGS TO BINS BY APPLYING SELF-ADHESIVE HOOKS TO THE SIDES OF THE TRASH BIN.

HAVING TROUBLE DECIDING ON WHAT TO ORDER? ASK FOR THE CHEF'S FAVORITE DISH.

REMOVE HIGHLIGHTER STAINS BY USING A LITTLE BIT OF LEMON JUICE ON A COTTON SWAB.

TYPING "(MONTH)(YEAR)" IN THE WIKIPEDIA SEARCH BAR WILL GIVE YOU THE MAJOR NEWS FOR THAT MONTH.

PLACING A MARSHMALLOW AT THE BOTTOM OF AN ICE CREAM CONE WILL HELP WITH DRIPPING.

Just stuff a marshmallow into the cone before adding your ice cream. As the ice cream melts, the marshmallow fills in the little gaps at the bottom of the cone, helping to keep everything inside.

STICK HALF OF A POOL NOODLE AGAINST THE WALL OF YOUR GARAGE TO PROTECT YOUR CAR DOORS FROM SLAMMING AGAINST THE WALL.

USE LEFTOVER COFFEE TO MAKE COFFEE ICE CUBES. THIS WILL HELP COOL DOWN COFFEE OR HELP KEEP AN ICED COFFEE FROM DILUTING.

POUR PANCAKE BATTER
OVER YOUR BACON TO
COOK A TWO-IN-ONE
BREAKFAST!

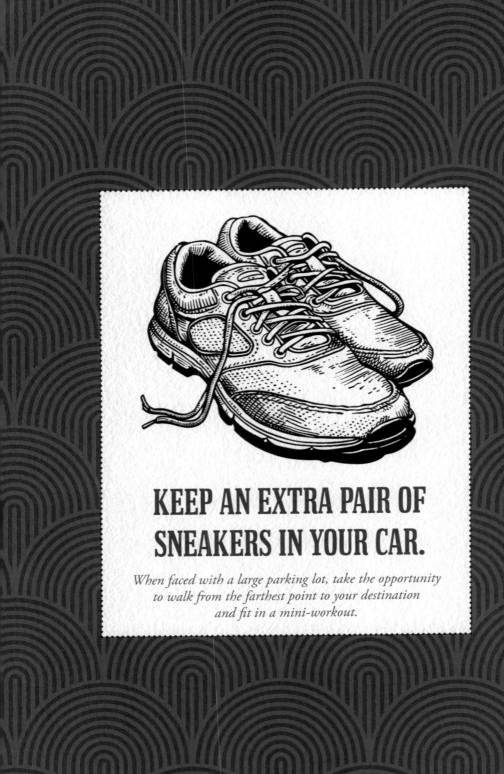

KEEP AN EXTRA PAIR OF SNEAKERS IN YOUR CAR.

When faced with a large parking lot, take the opportunity to walk from the farthest point to your destination and fit in a mini-workout.

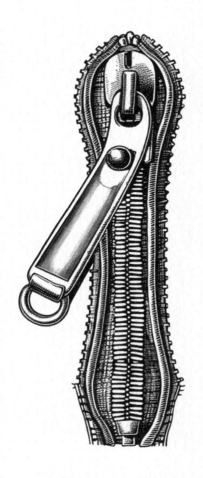

TO FREE A STUCK ZIPPER, TRY RUBBING A GRAPHITE PENCIL LEAD OVER THE TEETH.

The graphite in pencil lead naturally makes for an effective dry lubricant to get zippers unstuck. For best results, use a traditional wooden pencil instead of a mechanical version, as it's easier to get the graphite onto the zipper. Gently rub the pencil tip on both sides of the zipper teeth until you can see the graphite on the teeth.

USE INCOGNITO MODE WHEN BOOKING FLIGHTS AND HOTELS ONLINE FOR POTENTIALLY LOWER PRICES.

TAKE A STROLL OUTSIDE ON A SUNNY DAY FOR AN ENERGY BOOST!

USE AN ACCENTED LETTER AS A PART OF YOUR PASSWORD. NO ONE WILL EVER GUESS IT.

CLEAN TV AND COMPUTER SCREENS WITH COFFEE FILTERS TO AVOID SCRATCHES AND REDUCE STATIC.

SETTING A FAKE DEADLINE EARLIER THAN THE ACTUAL DEADLINE CAN HELP GIVE YOU A BUFFER IF THINGS TAKE LONGER OR IF SOMETHING GOES AWRY.

TO TRIM YOUR UTILITY BILLS, RUN MAJOR APPLIANCES LIKE DISHWASHERS OR LAUNDRY DRYERS OVERNIGHT.

If your utility company charges extra for peak usage times, a simple change to your routine can help. Using your non-essential appliances during off-peak hours instead can make a significant impact.

TAKE A HOT BATH OR SHOWER JUST
BEFORE BED. IT WILL HELP
YOU FEEL RELAXED.

PLACING YOUR LAPTOP ON TOP OF AN EMPTY EGG CARTON CAN HELP KEEP IT COOL.

Most laptops have a cooling system, but for various reasons they can sometimes overheat. Placing an egg carton under your laptop allows air to better circulate in and around the cups and under the laptop which helps it to cool.

USE EMPTY TISSUE BOXES TO STORE EXTRA TAKEOUT NAPKINS.

TO DISINFECT LEGOS AND OTHER SIMPLE PLASTIC TOYS, PUT THEM IN A LAUNDRY BAG AND RUN THEM THROUGH THE DISHWASHER.

USE DRYER SHEETS TO DUST SURFACES; THEY ATTRACT DUST AND LEAVE A FRESH SCENT.

TIRED OF EATING OUT? SAVE MONEY BY MAKING WEEKLY MEAL PLANS AND COOKING AT HOME.

DABBING THE STICKY PART OF A POST-IT NOTE CAN QUICKLY PICK UP ANY DIRT AND DUST FROM YOUR KEYBOARD.

USE MULTI-COLORED BINDER CLIPS TO SORT AND COLOR-CODE THE CORDS BEHIND YOUR TELEVISION OR COMPUTER.

USE AN BALLOON FILLED WITH TOOTHPASTE TO MAKE AN INEXPENSIVE STRESS BALL TO CALM YOUR NERVES.

MUFFIN TINS ARE A GREAT WAY TO KEEP SANDWICH AND BURGER CONDIMENTS SEPARATED.

USE A SLICE OF ONION TO CONTAIN YOUR FRIED EGG FOR THE PERFECTLY ROUND BREAKFAST SANDWICH.

CLOTHESPINS CAN HELP HOLD A NAIL WHILE HAMMERING.

All you need to do is hold the nail with a clothespin, hair pin or comb to prevent smashing fingers then pound into place with the hammer.

PLACING A SMALL TRACKER IN YOUR LUGGAGE OR ONTO YOUR KEY RING CAN HELP KEEP TRACK OF STUFF YOU LOSE OR ARE AFRAID TO LOSE!

MAYONNAISE CAN HELP REMOVE WATER STAINS AND RINGS ON FURNITURE.

The fat from the egg yolks and oil penetrates into the finish and replaces the moisture from the water stain. Meanwhile, the mild acidity from the vinegar helps break down the stain.

A FEW DROPS OF LEMON JUICE ON AVOCADOS AND GUACAMOLE WILL KEEP IT GREEN A LITTLE LONGER.

TRY USING YOUR STAND MIXER TO EASILY SHRED COOKED CHICKEN.

FLIPPING YOUR PEANUT BUTTER JAR UPSIDE DOWN WILL HELP KEEP THE OIL FROM SEPARATING.

FLIP A BUTTON—UP SHIRT INSIDE OUT TO IRON OVER THE BUTTON SIDE.

YOUR LOCAL PUBLIC LIBRARY HAS A WEALTH OF RESOURCES AT NO COST! STREAM MOVIES AND MUSIC FOR FREE!

DIRTY GROUT? USE A BLEACH PEN TO TARGET AND TRANSFORM YOUR STAINED GROUT.

PICK YOUR OUTFIT THE NIGHT BEFORE TO AVOID RUSHING TO PICK SOMETHING IN THE MORNING.

HANGING CLOTHES IN THE BATHROOM WHILE HAVING A HOT SHOWER WILL HELP STEAM AND UNWRINKLE THEM.

The steam from a hot shower can help loosen wrinkles naturally. Just hang the garment on a hanger or over the top of the door and let the steam do its work, either while you take a shower, or just turn the hot water on while you're out of it. The heat and steam help the fabric fibers relax, making wrinkles much easier to remove.

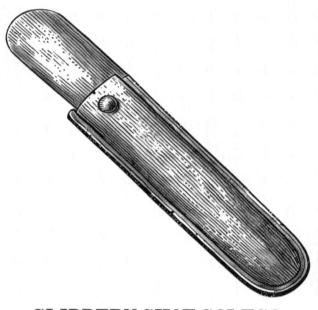

SLIPPERY SHOE SOLES? USE A NAIL FILE TO APPLY SOME TRACTION TO THE BOTTOMS.

One of the easiest, do-it-yourself ways to make your shoes slip-resistant is to scuff the soles with sandpaper, a nail file, or something else with a rough surface, such as brick, gravel or rock. Simply rub the rough item on the sole of your shoe until small grooves appear.

USE FROZEN GRAPES INSTEAD OF
ICE CUBES TO KEEP YOUR BEVERAGE
FROM BEING WATERED DOWN.

OUT OF SHAVING CREAM? USE CONDITIONER TO LATHER UP BEFORE SHAVING!

EATING AN APPLE CAN HELP YOU STAY AWAKE JUST AS CAFFEINE DOES.

Eating an apple is a healthy afternoon snack and is known to fight sleepiness. Best of all, there's no crash either.

REHEATING A PIZZA ON A FRYING PAN WILL HELP KEEP THE CRUST FROM GETTING SOGGY OR SOFT.

TAKE A PHOTO OF THE BACK OF ANY ELECTRONIC DEVICE WITH MULTIPLE WIRES OR CORDS TO REMEMBER THE SET UP IN CASE YOU EVER HAVE TO UNPLUG.

WORK IN A LOUD ENVIRONMENT? INVEST IN A PAIR OF NOISE-CANCELLING EARPHONES OR EARBUDS TO DROWN OUT THE NOISE.

READ YOUR FAVORITE BOOK AT LEAST ONCE A YEAR. YOU MIGHT GAIN A NEW PERSPECTIVE OF IT.

BEFORE FREEZING GROUND BEEF, PLACE IT IN A BAG AND FLATTEN IT OUT. THIS WILL HELP CUT THE TIME IT TAKES TO THAW.

FREEZING ALOE VERA IN AN ICE CUBE TRAY DURING THE SUMMER CAN HELP WITH THOSE PESKY SUNBURNS.

WRAPPING YOUR BANANA STEMS WITH PLASTIC OR CLING WRAP WILL HELP THEM STAY FRESH.

TOOTHPASTE CAN BE USED TO REMOVE CRAYON MARKS FROM WALLS.

Just grab some toothpaste and gently apply it to the crayon using a toothbrush. Scrub gently, then wipe with a clean, damp cloth.

TRAVELING WITH FRIENDS AND NEED TO SPLIT THE BILLS? USE MONEY-SHARING APPS TO TRANSFER FUNDS AMONG EACH OTHER.

DID YOU KNOW YOU CAN PLAY PAC-MAN BY SIMPLY TYPING IT INTO THE GOOGLE SEARCH BAR?

OUT OF CUP HOLDERS IN THE CAR?
TAKE OFF A SHOE AND PLACE YOUR
DRINK IN THE SHOE'S MOUTH.

USE BRIGHT SHADES OF NAIL
POLISH TO PAINT AND EASILY
DISTINGUISH YOUR KEYS.

NEVER SHOP AT A GROCERY STORE WHILE HUNGRY.

CANDLES LAST LONGER IF THEY ARE PLACED IN THE FREEZER A FEW HOURS BEFORE LIGHTING.

VELCRO STRIPS CAN BE USED TO KEEP YOUR RUGS IN PLACE.

HOLD A MEETING OUTDOORS DURING A NICE WEATHER DAY. A CHANGE IN SCENERY COULD BOOST PRODUCTIVITY AND MOOD.

HONEY IS AN EFFECTIVE COUGH SUPPRESSANT.

Studies show that honey may be an effective remedy to limit coughs. The thick texture of honey may help lower the urge to cough, by coating and soothing the throat.

ADD A PINCH OF SALT TO COFFEE GROUNDS TO ENHANCE FLAVOR AND REDUCE BITTERNESS.

CLEAN YOUR DRYER VENTS YEARLY TO PREVENT LINT BUILDUP.

STORING RAZOR BLADES IN BABY OIL WILL EXTEND THEIR USE.

FITTED SHEETS CAN BE A PAIN TO FIGURE OUT. THE TAG ON A FITTED SHEET FITS ONTO THE BOTTOM LEFT SIDE OR TOP RIGHT SIDE.

RUBBING CHAPSTICK OVER A PAPER CUT CAN HELP HEAL AND STOP THE PAIN.

The wax works to create a seal over the cut, so the bleeding slows and the pain diminishes because the nerves in your fingers aren't exposed to air anymore.

SPRINKLING BABY POWDER INSIDE YOUR SHOES CAN PREVENT THEM FROM SQUEAKING.

PLACING A PIECE OF CHALK IN YOUR TOOLBOX CAN HELP PREVENT TOOLS FROM RUSTING.

No need to stock up on anything fancy; a bundle of the typical blackboard stuff will do the trick. Then all you need to do is remember to switch in a new handful of chalk every few months.

USE NEWSPAPER INSTEAD OF PAPER TOWELS FOR A STREAK-FREE SHINE ON WINDOWS AND GLASS.

Newspapers are more absorbent than paper towels so they can soak up more liquid, which makes them ideal for wiping away residue from windows quickly and efficiently without leaving behind any smudges or streaks.

MAKE A NON-SLIP DOOR
STOP OUT OF A TENNIS BALL.

MAKE A DIY FACE MASK WITH YOGURT AND HONEY FOR MOISTURIZING BENEFITS.

Use a half cup to a whole cup of either plain yogurt or buttermilk and add 2 tablespoons of pure grade A honey. Mix together and apply to your face. The yogurt or buttermilk is good for evening out or even lightening the skin tone and the honey is a humectant which moisturizes. Leave it on for 10-15 minutes, then rinse well with warm water.

USE A CARABINER TO HOLD MULTIPLE BAGS OF GROCERIES.

TAKE A PHOTO OF YOUR PACKED SUITCASE'S ITEMS. THIS WILL HELP PROCESS ANY CLAIMS SHOULD AN AIRLINE LOSE YOUR LUGGAGE.

Take pictures and videos of the contents of your checked bags any time something valuable is inside. This is the best way to prove to the investigator handling the claim what was in your checked luggage.

ELIMINATE HAIR STATIC BY PUSHING A DRYER SHEET THROUGH THE BRUSH. BRUSH WITH THE SHEET INTACT.

USING A SPRING FROM A PEN CAN HELP KEEP A CORD FROM BENDING AND BREAKING.

PASSPORT PHOTOS CAN BE EXPENSIVE. USE TRAVEL.STATE. GOV AND THE CROP FEATURE TO MAKE YOUR OWN PHOTO.

BUY A CAR AT THE END OF THE MONTH. SALESPEOPLE ARE LIKELY TO GIVE YOU A BETTER DEAL AS THEY ARE TRYING TO MEET THEIR MONTHLY QUOTAS.

TRY STANDING UP EVERY 30 MINUTES WHEN WORKING AT YOUR DESK. STANDING HELPS WITH BLOOD FLOW AND ENERGY LEVELS.

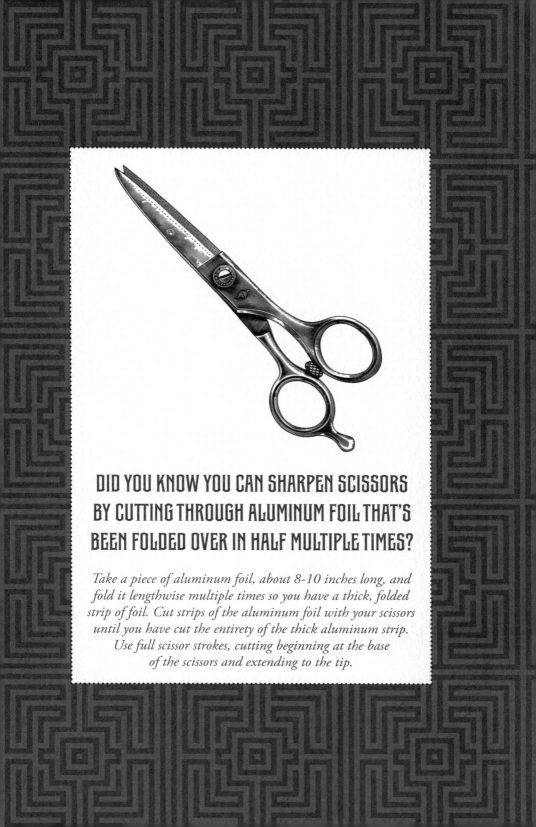

DID YOU KNOW YOU CAN SHARPEN SCISSORS BY CUTTING THROUGH ALUMINUM FOIL THAT'S BEEN FOLDED OVER IN HALF MULTIPLE TIMES?

Take a piece of aluminum foil, about 8-10 inches long, and fold it lengthwise multiple times so you have a thick, folded strip of foil. Cut strips of the aluminum foil with your scissors until you have cut the entirety of the thick aluminum strip. Use full scissor strokes, cutting beginning at the base of the scissors and extending to the tip.

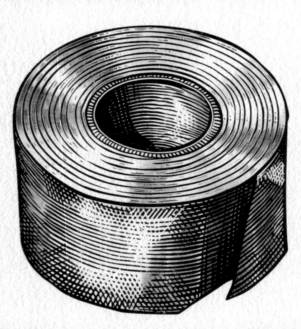

USING DUCT TAPE IS AN EFFECTIVE WAY OF PICKING UP PET HAIR LEFT ON THE COUCH.

YOU CAN USE AN ICE CUBE TRAY TO ORGANIZE EARRINGS AND OTHER SMALL JEWELRY ITEMS.

PLAN OUT YOUR ENTIRE WEEK ON THE WEEKENDS. MAKING A LIST OF TO-DO ITEMS CAN HELP KEEP YOU AND YOUR SCHEDULE ON TASK.

USE SHAVING CREAM TO CLEAN A DIRTY MIRROR.

HAVE A HARD TIME KEEPING TRACK OF BILLS? SET THEM TO AUTO-PAY SO THAT YOU NEVER MISS A DUE DATE.

STICK A POST-IT NOTE UNDER A DRILL SPOT BEFORE DRILLING. THE POST-IT WILL HELP CATCH DUST AND DEBRIS.

PLACING YOUR PHONE OR ALARM CLOCK AWAY FROM YOUR BED WILL HELP YOU GET OUT OF BED IN THE MORNING.

Never ever put your phone within arm's reach of your bed. You want to force yourself to get out of bed and walk over to your phone to turn it off.

TYING A KNOT AROUND WIRED EARPHONES CAN HELP YOU DISTINGUISH WHICH BUD IS FOR THE LEFT OR RIGHT EAR.

BATCHING TOGETHER SIMILAR TASKS CAN HELP YOU TACKLE THEM IN AN EFFICIENT MANNER.

HANGERS WITH CLIPS CAN BE ALSO USED AS CHIP CLIPS!

MIRRORING ANOTHER PERSON'S BODY LANGUAGE CAN HELP IN BUILDING TRUST WITH THAT PERSON.

PUSHING THE END OF A CHOPSTICK THROUGH A CHERRY CAN TAKE OUT ALL OF THOSE PESKY PITS!

Sit a cherry over the mouth of an empty soda, beer, or wine bottle—the sturdier, the better. Steady the cherry and push a chopstick or metal straw in the top of the stemmed cherry until you feel the pit. Keep pushing down to force the pit out of the bottom of the cherry and into the empty bottle.

USING THE END OF A PAPER CLIP CAN HELP CLEAN YOUR PHONE JACK. GENTLY USE THE END TO DIG OUT DUST AND DEBRIS.

UNWRINKLE YOUR CLOTHES BY THROWING ICE CUBES IN THE DRYER ALONG WITH YOUR CLOTHES. THE ICE CUBES HELP CREATE A STEAM AS THE DRYER HEATS UP.

**DON'T HAVE A TOOTHBRUSH CONTAINER?
USE A WATER BOTTLE.**

ADDING A PIECE OF BREAD IN AN AIRTIGHT CONTAINER CAN HELP KEEP COOKIES SOFT AND FRESH!

When you pack cookies away in a container or storage bag, toss in a slice of any kind of bread before sealing them up. Basically, the cookies will absorb moisture from the bread, which keeps them nice and soft.

SELF–CARE IS A MINDSET, NOT AN ITEM ON A TO–DO LIST.

WHEN USING A PUBLIC RESTROOM, USE THE INNER SIDE OF THE TOILET PAPER.

TAPE ADHESIVE CAN BE REMOVED BY SPRAYING A LITTLE WD-40 AND WIPING AWAY THE RESIDUE.

Use a terry cloth with a bit of texture to it and soak a small area of it with WD-40. If there is a lot of residue, you can spray the residue and let it sit for just a minute before scrubbing.

RUNNING A FINE-TOOTH COMB OVER A WOOL SWEATER OR FLEECE WILL KEEP IT LOOKING NEW.

USE BROTH IN YOUR BOXED MAC 'N' CHEESE IF YOU'RE OUT OF MILK.

A DRYER SHEET CAN KEEP MOSQUITOES AWAY. KEEP ONE HANDY NEAR YOU OR IN A POCKET WHEN OUTDOORS.

PLACE A WOODEN SPOON OVER A POT OF BOILING WATER TO KEEP IT FROM SPILLING OVER.

The wood acts as a water repellant on the already-unstable bubbles. As a result, it causes them to destabilize and stop rising. Also, the spoon is at a cooler temperature than the water and bubbles, so when the bubbles meet the spoon, the steam condenses back into the water.

JOIN A GYM IN THE SUMMER MONTHS
RATHER THAN JANUARY. GYMS TEND TO
RUN PROMOTIONS DURING WARMER MONTHS
WHEN WORKOUTS ARE POPULAR OUTDOORS.

PLACING CUPCAKE PAPER THROUGH
YOUR POPSICLE STICK WILL KEEP
THE MELTING CONTAINED!

SHOWER CURTAIN RINGS CAN DOUBLE AS PURSE HANGERS IN YOUR CLOSET.

USE SEAT WARMERS IN YOUR CAR TO KEEP YOUR PIZZA AND TAKEOUT WARM ON THE WAY HOME.

WRAPPING YOUR CHEESE IN PARCHMENT PAPER WILL HELP KEEP IT FRESH.

SHOP FOR HOME AND AUTO INSURANCE ANNUALLY. GETTING A QUOTE IS EASY AND COULD HELP YOU SAVE!

RUNNING WARM WATER OVER A HARD-TO-TWIST LID CAN HELP LOOSEN IT UP.

The heat can help the metal expand a bit, making it easier to break the seal as it loses its grip on the edge of the jar.

A SOUND MACHINE CAN HELP DROWN OUT THE NOISE OF FOOTSTEPS FROM YOUR UPSTAIRS NEIGHBOR.

CLEAN YOUR BLENDER HANDS-FREE BY PUTTING SOAP AND WATER INTO THE BLENDER AND TURNING IT ON FOR A FEW SECONDS.

TRY LIMITING YOUR EMAILS TO A MAXIMUM OF FIVE SENTENCES.

This can help keep things short and to-the-point and cut down on the amount of time you spend writing.

TO RIPEN AVOCADOS QUICKLY, PLACE THEM IN A PAPER BAG WITH A BANANA AND LEAVE OVERNIGHT.

SPRINKLE A LITTLE SALT INTO YOUR PAN BEFORE FRYING SOMETHING. THIS SHOULD HELP PREVENT THE OIL FROM SPLATTERING AS IT HEATS.

Sprinkle a bit of salt in the hot oil when it starts to bubble. It will absorb moisture from food, preventing splashing.

POUR PANCAKE BATTER INTO AN EMPTY KETCHUP OR CONDIMENT BOTTLE FOR A NICE PANCAKE WITHOUT THE MESS!

USE A CHOPSTICK TO
TEST OIL TEMPERATURE.

*Dip the end of a wooden spoon or chopstick in the oil and
if the oil starts sizzling and bubbling around the stick,
the oil is hot. The faster and more furious the bubbles,
the hotter the oil. If the oil starts smoking, it's too
hot—adjust the heat and then check again.*

USE WHITE RICE TO CLEAN OUT A SPICE OR COFFEE GRINDER. SIMPLY PULSE WHITE RICE TO ABSORB LOOSE SPICES (AND SMELLS!).

POKING A FORK THROUGH THE CREAM PART OF AN OREO COOKIE CAN HELP KEEP THE MESS AWAY.

PLACING A PAPER TOWEL
IN A BAG OR CONTAINER
OF SALAD WILL HELP
ABSORB MOISTURE TO
KEEP YOUR LEAFY GREENS
FROM GETTING SOGGY.

PACKING SHOES FOR A TRIP?
PLACE THEM IN A SHOWER
CAP TO KEEP YOUR LUGGAGE
AND CLOTHING CLEAN
WHEN PACKING!

STORING YOUR FOLDED BED
SHEETS, PILLOWCASES,
AND LIGHTER BEDDING IN A
PILLOWCASE WILL KEEP IT
ALL TOGETHER AND TIDY.

RUN A SPOON
UNDER HOT WATER
BEFORE SCOOPING
ICE CREAM.

MAKE COPIES OF IMPORTANT DOCUMENTS SUCH AS PASSPORTS, IDS, AND BIRTH
CERTIFICATES. THESE COPIES CAN BE HANDY WHEN TRYING TO REPLACE THEM.

IF YOU NEED TO FILL UP A BUCKET THAT WON'T FIT UNDER YOUR SINK'S FAUCET, USE A POOL NOODLE AS A HOSE.

WHETHER YOU LIKE TO DECORATE OR NOT, PLACING A FEW ITEMS THAT BELONG TO YOU CAN MAKE ALL THE DIFFERENCE IN HELPING YOUR WORKSPACE FEEL LIKE YOURS.

WHEN YOU MEET SOMEONE NEW, SAY THEIR NAME OUT LOUD AT SOME POINT IN THE CONVERSATION. YOU'RE MORE LIKELY TO REMEMBER IT BY SAYING IT.

KEEP UNUSED GARDEN SEEDS IN AN AIRTIGHT CONTAINER WITH A SILICA PACK TO KEEP THEM FRESH AND USABLE FOR THE NEXT YEAR.

It's essential that the seeds remain dry while being stored. To soak up any moisture, place a silica gel packet in your glass jar and replace it every six months. You can also keep seeds dry using rice kernels.

WHEN YOU FEEL A SNEEZE COMING, PINCH YOUR NOSE JUST ABOVE THE NOSTRILS, AND THE SNEEZE WILL GO AWAY.

CUT AND DECORATE CEREAL BOXES TO USE AS MAGAZINE OR DOCUMENT ORGANIZERS.

MASSAGE YOUR SCALP WITH
ESSENTIAL OILS TO PROMOTE
HAIR GROWTH.

WRAP A WET PAPER TOWEL AROUND YOUR BEVERAGE BEFORE PUTTING IT IN THE FREEZER. YOU'LL HAVE A CHILLED BEVERAGE 15 MINUTES LATER.

SOAK A CHEESECLOTH IN BUTTER AND DRAPE OVER TURKEY TO KEEP IT MOIST WHILE ROASTING.

Melt one stick of butter and soak the cheesecloth in the melted butter. Place the soaked cheesecloth on top of the turkey, put in the oven and ignore it until it is finished cooking.

STRETCHING BEFORE GOING TO SLEEP CAN AID IN RELAXING YOUR MUSCLES.

CLOSE YOUR OFFICE DOOR WHEN YOU NEED TO DO WORK. THIS CAN HELP SEND A SIGNAL TO CO-WORKERS THAT YOU ARE BUSY AND SHOULD NOT BE DISTURBED.

A STAPLE REMOVER CAN BE USED TO WEDGE THOSE HARD TO SEPARATE KEY RINGS.

STORE TOILET PAPER IN COFFEE CANS TO KEEP IT DRY ON CAMPING TRIPS.

AFTER CUTTING ONIONS OR GARLIC ON A CUTTING BOARD, APPLY LEMON TO THE BOARD TO NEUTRALIZE THE ODOR.

Cut a lemon in half and "scrub" it across your cutting board in a circular motion. It will sanitize your cutting board and the acid in the lemon will get rid of the smell.

MANY AIRPORTS HAVE MULTIPLE SECURITY CHECKPOINTS. IF ONE LOOKS FULL, TRY WALKING A LITTLE BIT FARTHER TO ANOTHER CHECKPOINT.

HAVE A LITTLE BIT OF NUTELLA LEFT IN YOUR JAR? ADD ICE CREAM AND MIX TO CREATE A DELICIOUS TREAT!

USE COOKING SPRAY ON SNOW SHOVELS TO PREVENT SNOW FROM STICKING.

Removing stuck snow on your shovel can take a lot of extra time. To avoid the extra hassle, spray your shovel with cooking spray, spread vegetable oil or coat it in wax. The spray or oil will act as a lubricant, preventing the snow from sticking to the shovel.

USE A BUDGET APP TO HELP WITH FINANCES.

ABSORB GREASE SPILLS WITH CORNMEAL.

VOLUNTEERING WITH LOCAL NONPROFITS CAN HELP YOUR MENTAL HEALTH AND HELP YOU NETWORK WITH LIKE-MINDED PEOPLE IN YOUR COMMUNITY.

COLLECT TINY GLASS SHARDS WITH A PIECE OF BREAD.

Simply press a slice of soft bread against the small pieces until they stick and dispose of the bread.

WRAP RUBBER BANDS AT THE ENDS OF CLOTHES HANGERS TO KEEP GARMENTS FROM SLIPPING.

USING SMART LIGHTING CAN HELP DETER BURGLARS FROM TARGETING YOUR HOUSE. SET THE LIGHTS ON A TIMER TO MAKE IT APPEAR YOU ARE HOME WHILE YOU ARE TRAVELING OR AWAY.

CREATE A QUICK BAIN-MARIE BY PLACING A METAL BOWL OVER A POT OF SIMMERING WATER.

This could be a metal mixing bowl, a glass Pyrex dish, or a small saucepan. Make sure the container fits snugly over the pot of simmering water. Place the container of food over the pot of simmering water. The bottom of the container should not touch the water.

POURING COLA INTO A TOILET AND LETTING IT SIT OVERNIGHT, CAN HELP CLEAN DIRTY TOILETS.

Turn off the water supply behind the toilet. Flush to empty the bowl of water. Fill your toilet bowl with a two-liter bottle of cola and let sit overnight.

CRAMPS? DRINK A LITTLE BIT OF PICKLE JUICE AND THEY'LL GO AWAY.

Pickle juice for cramps is thought to work because it stimulates a neuromuscular reflex that tells your brain to release a muscle cramp. Pickle juice may be particularly effective at triggering this cramp-relieving reflex due to its combination of salt and acetic acid.

BILL INCREASE? LOWER YOUR INTERNET OR CABLE BILLS BY SPEAKING TO A RETENTION DEPARTMENT.

DISINFECT AND DEODORIZE A MATTRESS WITH VODKA SPRAY.

Pour the vodka into a spray bottle and then lightly spray to cover all surfaces of the mattress with the vodka without soaking. You may want to dilute the vodka if it's too powerful. Optional: Add a few drops of your favorite essential oil to the vodka solution to leave your mattress smelling fresh and inviting.

USE A POTATO TO UNSCREW A BROKEN LIGHT BULB SAFELY.

PLACE A PIECE OF TAPE OVER THE SPEAKER OF NOISY TOYS TO REDUCE THE VOLUME.

CHILL GUM ON FABRIC WITH AN ICE CUBE TO EASILY SCRAPE IT OFF.

To harden the gum and easily remove it from your clothing, try rubbing the affected area with an ice cube. Once it's hardened, remove it swiftly with a butter knife or scraper.

FREEZE A WET SPONGE INSIDE A ZIP-LOCK BAG FOR A HOMEMADE ICE PACK.

USE A COLANDER TO EVENLY DISTRIBUTE POPCORN TOPPINGS.

ORGANIZE SPICES IN A DRAWER WITH ANGLED ORGANIZERS FOR EASY VIEWING.

STORE SEASONAL CLOTHING IN VACUUM SEAL BAGS TO SAVE SPACE.

TURN A LADDER SIDEWAYS FOR AN INSTANT WARDROBE OR STORAGE SOLUTION.

EVER NOTICE THE STAR NEXT TO A CERTAIN FLOOR ON AN ELEVATOR? THAT STAR INDICATES WHICH FLOOR LEADS OUTSIDE.

USE A PLASTIC BOTTLE TO SEPARATE EGG YOLKS FROM WHITES.

Use an empty plastic bottle to separate egg yolks. Just squeeze the bottle, place opening on yolk and let suction do the work.

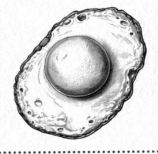

PUT A CUP OF WATER IN THE DISHWASHER FOR BETTER HEAT DISTRIBUTION DURING DRYING.

USE A PIZZA CUTTER TO EASILY CUT HERBS.

*To cut fresh, leafy herbs such as cilantro and parsley, use
a pizza wheel rather than a knife—just run the wheel over
the washed leaves in multiple directions. The wheel also
prevents bruising the leaves, a common problem
when mincing with a knife.*

SAVE MONEY BY BUYING GENERIC OR STORE
BRANDS RATHER THAN NAME BRANDS.

USE A PAPER CLIP ON THE BACK OF THE BRA TO HIDE THE STRAPS.

APPLY VASELINE ON PULSE POINTS BEFORE SPRAYING PERFUME OR COLOGNE TO MAKE THE SCENT LAST LONGER.

Pulse points encompass the warmer areas of your body such as your wrists, inner elbows, neck and the back of your knees that can help diffuse fragrance.

TURN ON TWO-FACTOR AUTHENTICATION FOR YOUR IMPORTANT ACCOUNTS.

WHEN YOU TRAVEL PACK A SMALL FIRST-AID KIT WITH ESSENTIALS LIKE BAND-AIDS AND PAIN RELIEVERS.

TAKE A WEEKEND EACH MONTH TO EXPLORE YOUR OWN COMMUNITY. YOU'LL FIND ATTRACTIONS, STORES, AND RESTAURANTS YOU NEVER KNEW EXISTED!

INSTALL A TENSION ROD UNDER THE SINK FOR HANGING SPRAY BOTTLES.

DILUTE APPLE CIDER VINEGAR WITH WATER FOR A DIY TONER.

USE A MEAT TENDERIZER TO CRUSH NUTS OR CANDIES.

USE A PILL ORGANIZER TO CARRY SMALL AMOUNTS OF SPICES FOR COOKING ON THE GO.

PLACE A CUP OF WATER IN THE MICROWAVE WITH PIZZA TO KEEP THE CRUST FROM GETTING CHEWY.

Put a microwave-safe glass of water in the microwave right next to your pizza. Heat it up for about 45 seconds and your pizza should look and taste identical to how the pizza guy delivered it to you last night.

TURN YOUR SMARTPHONE INTO A REMOTE CONTROL FOR YOUR COMPUTER OR TV.

CARRY A REUSABLE WATER BOTTLE AND REFILL IT AFTER AIRPORT SECURITY.

PESKY FRUIT FLIES CAN BE GONE WITH A SMALL GLASS OF APPLE CIDER VINEGAR AND DISH SOAP.

Pour about half an inch of apple cider vinegar into a bowl or jar. Add a drop of dish soap to the container with vinegar. The dish soap will break the surface tension of the apple cider vinegar, causing the fruit flies to sink when they land on it.

5 GALLON BUCKETS STUCK TOGETHER?
USE COMPRESSED AIR TO GET THEM APART.
JUST STICK YOUR AIR COMPRESSOR
NOZZLE IN BETWEEN THEM AND
THEY WILL COME APART.

MIX A SMALL AMOUNT OF PEPPERMINT OIL INTO YOUR LIP GLOSS TO PLUMP YOUR LIPS.

Peppermint oil is often used in lip plumping products due to its natural ability to stimulate blood flow to the lips, creating a temporary plumping effect. However, it's important to note that essential oils can be very potent and may cause irritation or allergic reactions in some individuals. It's always best to dilute essential oils properly before using them on the skin and to perform a patch test to check for any adverse reactions.

SAVE ON DATA ROAMING CHARGES BY DOWNLOADING AREAS ON GOOGLE MAPS FOR OFFLINE USE.

STORE GINGER IN THE FREEZER TO MAKE IT EASIER TO GRATE.

MIX LOOSE PIGMENTS WITH PETROLEUM JELLY TO MAKE YOUR OWN CUSTOM LIP GLOSS.

PACK CLOTHES IN COLOR SCHEMES THAT MIX AND MATCH WELL TO MAXIMIZE OUTFIT COMBINATIONS.

USE NON-GEL TOOTHPASTE ON PIMPLES TO REDUCE REDNESS OVERNIGHT.

USE THE TV'S USB PORT TO CHARGE DEVICES IF YOU FORGET THE WALL PLUG.

SOAK SKEWERS IN WATER BEFORE GRILLING TO PREVENT BURNING.

Wooden skewers, like the classic bamboo skewers, can burn easily over a hot grill. Soaking them in warm water for 10 to 30 minutes before threading will keep the skewers from cooking along with the food.

PUTTING GROUND COFFEE ON VOMIT WILL HELP TAKE AWAY THE SMELL AND DEHYDRATE IT. THIS WILL MAKE IT EASIER TO CLEAN UP.

USE A BANANA PEEL TO POLISH SILVERWARE.

ORGANIZE YOUR DIGITAL FILES WITH A CONSISTENT NAMING CONVENTION AND FOLDER STRUCTURE.

MONITOR YOUR HOME'S ENERGY USE WITH A SMART METER.

PACK A POWER STRIP TO CHARGE MULTIPLE DEVICES IN HOTELS WITH LIMITED OUTLETS.

USE A TEA BAG TO FIX A BROKEN NAIL.

Trim a piece of a tea bag to sufficiently cover the area surrounding the split. Apply nail glue to the nail, adding a little extra over the split itself. Using tweezers, place the tea bag piece on the nail. Then, coat the tea bag piece with additional nail glue, ensuring the split is fully covered.

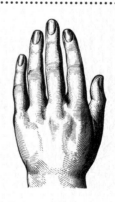

WRAP BREAKABLE ITEMS IN CLOTHES AND PLACE THEM IN THE CENTER OF YOUR SUITCASE.

USE THE HOTEL'S BUSINESS CARD TO REMEMBER YOUR HOTEL ADDRESS OR TO SHOW TAXI DRIVERS.

TURN A PENCIL EYELINER INTO A GEL FORMULA WITH THE HELP OF A LIGHTER OR MATCH.

ROLL CITRUS FRUITS BEFORE JUICING TO MAXIMIZE JUICE OUTPUT.

WEAR YOUR HEAVIEST CLOTHES AND SHOES ON THE FLIGHT TO SAVE LUGGAGE SPACE.

REDUCE EYE STRAIN WITH MONITOR CALIBRATION TOOLS.

Proper monitor calibration plays a crucial role in preventing eye strain and maximizing visual comfort. By adjusting the contrast, brightness and color temperature of your display to optimal levels, you can minimize eye fatigue and discomfort.

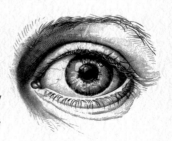

PUT VANILLA EXTRACT IN THE OVEN FOR A FEW MINUTES FOR A SWEET-SMELLING HOUSE.

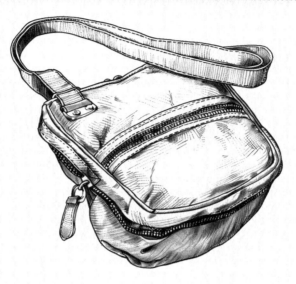

WHEN TRAVELING, BRING A SMALL, FOLDABLE DAY PACK FOR DAY TRIPS OR EXTRA PURCHASES.

A light, foldable backpack is ideal as it fits inside your main bags on travel days. It also allows you to travel with just one carry-on bag but still have a small bag for exploring. A collapsible daypack is also useful when you don't need a bag for the whole day.

USE A WAFFLE IRON TO MAKE QUICK
OMELETS OR HASH BROWNS.

KEEP A DRY ERASE MARKER IN THE KITCHEN TO NOTE EXPIRATION DATES ON CONTAINERS.

PLACE YOUR CREAMS IN THE FRIDGE FOR A COOLING EFFECT THAT HELPS REDUCE PUFFINESS.

CUSTOMIZE YOUR DEVICE'S POWER-SAVING MODE SETTINGS TO EXTEND BATTERY LIFE.

RUN A CRAYON OVER SCRATCHES IN FURNITURE TO FILL AND BLEND THEM.

Rub the crayon over the scratched area both sideways and lengthways until the scratch is full of wax. Use an old loyalty or credit card to gently scrape away any excess wax off the surface.

CARRY SNACKS LIKE NUTS OR GRANOLA BARS TO AVOID BUYING OVERPRICED AIRPORT FOOD.

AUTOMATE YOUR SAVINGS WITH APPS THAT ROUND UP PURCHASES TO THE NEAREST DOLLAR.

SOURCES

Page 5: https://www.readytechgo.com.au/boost-your-phones-speaker-volume-with-just-a-cup

Page 9: https://www.sleepfoundation.org/napping

Page 10: https://www.classicdrycleaner.com/removing-wrinkles-in-clothing

Page 22: https://yardandgarden.extension.iastate.edu/faq/can-i-manage-weeds-boiling-water

Page 23: https://www.familyhandyman.com/article/the-miracle-of-a-walnut

Page 26: https://www.everydayhealth.com/water-health/water-body-health.aspx

Page 28: https://www.quora.com/How-does-the-envelope-method-or-cash-stuffing-help-young-adults-stay-on-budget

Page 29: https://www.wikihow.com/Shave-With-Olive-Oil

Page 30: https://www.sensodyne.com/en-us/oral-health-tips/gum-health/brush-or-floss-first

Page 33: https://www.usps.com/manage/hold-mail.htm

Page 34: https://www.quora.com/Will-a-full-fridge-or-empty-fridge-consume-more-energy

Page 35: https://www.thespruce.com/reasons-to-make-your-bed-every-day-350511

Page 38: https://www.forbes.com/sites/amyblaschka/2020/09/21/this-is-why-you-need-to-turn-off-social-media-notifications

Page 39: https://happyegg.com/eggs/how-to-peel-hard-boiled-eggs

Page 42: https://www.thedailymeal.com/1295679/marshmallow-hack-delightfully-drip-free-ice-cream-cones

Page 45: https://www.stitchfix.com/women/blog/ask-a-stylist/how-to-get-zipper-unstuck

Page 46: https://www.we-energies.com/services/time-of-use

Page 48: https://www.housedigest.com/1545070/egg-carton-home-office-hack-cool-laptop-over-heating

Page 50: https://www.homehacks.com/hold-nail-with-clothes-pin-hair-pin-or-comb-to-prevent-smashing-fingers

Page 51: https://todayshomeowner.com/furniture/guides/how-to-remove-water-stains-from-furniture-with-mayonnaise

Page 54: https://www.connersappliance.com/blog/remove-wrinkles-from-clothes

Page 55: https://www.shoezone.com/Blog/how-to-make-shoes-less-slippery

Page 61: https://www.goodrx.com/conditions/cough/does-honey-help-cough

Page 62: https://www.healthdigest.com/1340550/fix-papercut-woes-easy-chapstick-hack

Page 63: https://hellamaid.ca/cleaning-guide/cleaning-windows-with-newspaper

Page 65: https://www.mindbodygreen.com/articles/all-natural-moisturizers-you-can-find-in-the-kitchen

Page 66: https://thepointsguy.com/news/take-photos-videos-of-suitcase-contents

Page 67: https://einatkessler.com/keep-scissors-sharp

Page 70: https://food52.com/hotline/15324-how-to-pit-cherries-efficiently-without-a-cherry-pitter

Page 72: https://www.purewow.com/food/how-to-keep-cookies-soft

Page 73: https://echotape.com/adhesive-tape/ten-simple-solutions-to-remove-tape-residue

Page 74: https://www.southernliving.com/food/kitchen-assistant/how-to-keep-water-from-boiling-over

SOURCES

Page 78: https://borges1896.com/blog/tip-avoid-splattering-oil

Page 79: https://myfoodstory.com/deep-frying-oil-temperature

Page 82: https://homesteadgardens.com/how-to-store-leftover-seeds-for-next-years-garden-season

Page 86: https://au.lifestyle.yahoo.com/why-rock-block-fans-were-154400595.html

Page 88: https://www.accuweather.com/en/winter-weather/how-cooking-spray-and-socks-can-make-shoveling-snow-easier/335834

Page 90: https://www.bakeonkit.com/post/how-to-make-a-bain-marie-blog

Page 91: https://www.today.com/home/clean-your-toilet-coca-cola-plus-4-other-genius-spring-t119479

Page 92: https://www.onepeloton.com/blog/pickle-juice-for-cramps

Page 93: https://www.ghostbed.com/pages/how-to-disinfect-and-sanitize-your-mattress

Page 95: https://www.cuisineathome.com/tips/pizza-herb-and-lettuce-cutter

Page 97: https://www.southernliving.com/does-vaseline-make-perfume-last-longer-7565444

Page 98: https://spoonuniversity.com/lifestyle/how-to-reheat-pizza-in-the-microwave

Page 99: https://www.orkin.com/pests/flies/fruit-flies/apple-cider-vinegar-fruit-fly-traps

Page 101: https://www.quora.com/Can-peppermint-essential-oil-be-used-to-plump-up-the-lips

Page 103: https://www.seriouseats.com/best-metal-bamboo-skewers-grilling-equipment

Page 105: https://www.cosmopolitan.com/uk/beauty-hair/beauty-trends/a43384527/how-to-fix-a-broken-nail

Page 106: https://www.displaycalibration.de/en/monitor-calibration-for-eye-strain-prevention-what-you-need-to-know

Page 107: https://www.neverendingvoyage.com/best-packable-daypack-travel

Page 109: https://www.gathered.how/homes-diy/home-repairs/how-to-remove-scratches-from-wooden-furniture